Hop on the Bus

Written by Helen Dineen

Collins

It is a bus map.

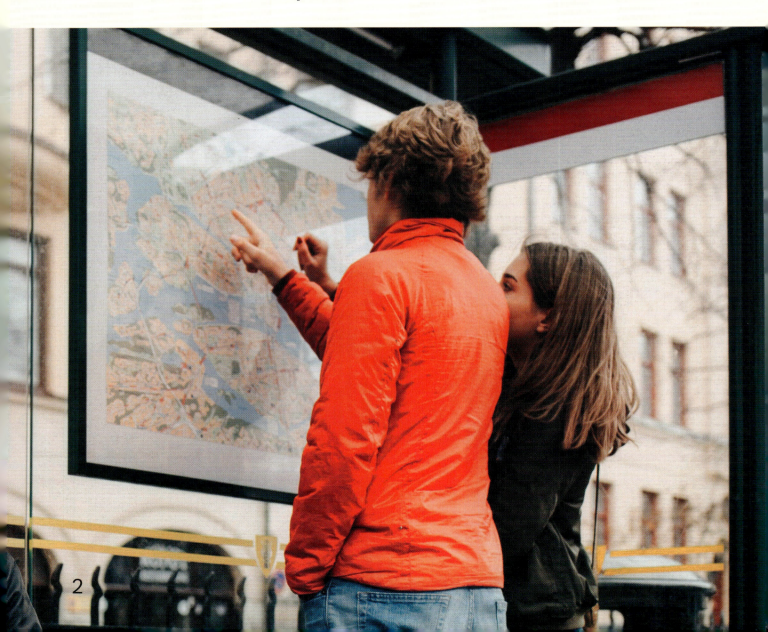

It is the bus.

The bus is big.

The bus is red.

Hop on the bus.

Sit on the top deck.

Get on the bus.

The bus sets off.

A dog is on the bus.

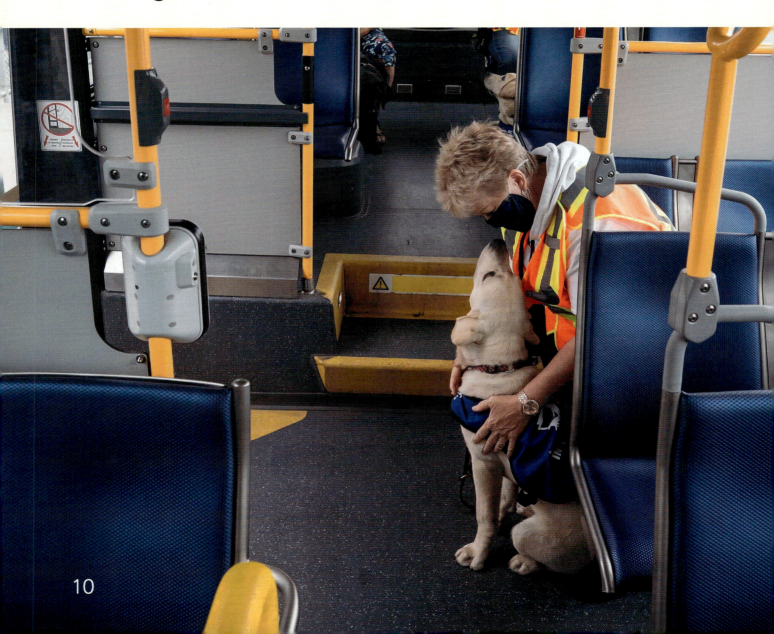

Get up. Hit the bell.

Hop off the bus.

It is fun on the bus!

15

 Review: After reading

Use your assessment from hearing the children read to choose any GPCs, words or tricky words that need additional practice.

Read 1: Decoding

- Ask the children to read page 9. Focus on the meaning of the phrase **sets off**. Ask: What other words could we use that mean the same? (e.g. *goes, gets going, starts*)
- Ask the children to read page 6. Ask them to point to the /h/ sound. (*hop*) Ask the children to read page 11, encouraging them to blend in their heads, silently, before reading the words aloud. Ask: Where is the /h/ sound? (*hit*)
- Look at the "I spy sounds" pages (14–15) together. Point to a fish, and say "fish", emphasising the /f/ sound. Ask the children to find items in the picture that start with the /f/ sound. (e.g. *five, flowers, fire, football, flies, fairy, frog, flamingo, fruit*)

Read 2: Prosody

- Focus on the exclamation mark.
- Read page 13. Ask the children to find the exclamation mark. Talk about how exclamation marks often show we need to read the words with extra expression.
- Read the text on page 13 twice – once with a very flat, unemotional tone, and once with more expression and enthusiasm. Ask the children which reading they prefer. Encourage them to practise reading the text with appropriate expression.

Read 3: Comprehension

- Discuss buses and what it is like to travel in one. Ask: Where would you sit on a bus? Why? What noises might you hear? Do you think being on a bus is fun? Why?
- Talk about what you do before, during and at the end of a bus ride. Prompt with questions, for example ask:
  - on page 2: What might you do before you get on a bus? (e.g. *look at a map*)
  - on page 7: Can you choose where to sit? (e.g. *yes, you can choose to be on the top deck*)
  - on page 11: What might you do before you get off? Why? (*hit the bell to tell the driver you want the bus to stop*)